Avoiding Plagiarism:
The Easy Way!
Writing with Honesty and Integrity

Peggy M. Houghton, Ph.D.
Timothy J. Houghton, Ph.D.

Editor: Pamela A. Presnal

Education is one of the best investments you will ever make . . . and our books maximize that investment!

Houghton & Houghton

ISBN 13: 978-1-7330079-1-7

ISBN 10: 1-7330079-1-1

For more information, contact:

www.kendallhunt.com
Send all inquiries to:
4050 Westmark Drive
Dubuque, IA 52004-1840

Table of Contents

Plagiarism Introduction

What is plagiarism in education?

Plagiarism is a form of academic dishonesty. Essentially, it entails using other people's thoughts and ideas without giving them proper credit as the original source. Students who plagiarize make it appear as if the work they have submitted for an assignment is their own, when in reality it is the work of someone else.

What is in this guide?

This guide is designed to help students avoid plagiarism. It contains real examples of students who failed courses for violations of academic honesty.

This book is not based on research or theory; it is based on actual experiences from two professors who have been involved in academia for over 40 years and graded thousands of student papers. We explain the basics of plagiarism as simply as possible, give real examples of plagiarized work, and show how to avoid academic dishonesty in writing. We understand what it takes to write quality papers using proper citation of deserving authors, and so will you after reading this book. That being said, we still suggest you consult your college or university about rules regarding academic honesty since they might have specific requirements that go above and beyond those covered in this guide.

Also included are examples of properly citing authors of books and journals in the reference section of the papers you compose. These examples include APA and MLA writing styles. This is very valuable information that will help you throughout your educational and working career because APA and MLA are used worldwide for academic and non-academic writing.

Why do you need this guide?

If you are a college student who is unfamiliar with the dangers of plagiarism, then this book is a must for you! Many universities do not tolerate academic dishonesty, and ignorance is not an excuse. Quite simply, you do not want to jeopardize a grade due to a misunderstanding of academic honesty.

Keep in mind that plagiarism can result in a failing grade, and a failing grade can produce a plethora of negative consequences including:

1. *You will lose credit for the course*—Those credits need to be made up in order to graduate, and that costs money. Some tuition exceeds $400 per credit hour, so failing a 4 credit course could cost you over $1600. If you are on scholarship, the scholarship might not pay for the same course twice, or it might only pay for a certain number of credits regardless of whether you pass or fail. If you are taking out loans to pay for college, you will accrue more debt. If your parents or other people are paying for your college, they will be forced to pay more.

2. *You might need to repeat the same course*—Some courses are required for graduation in certain majors. If you need to complete the course you failed, you will have to repeat it. It can be very frustrating doing the same work twice. It's like losing a paper on your hard drive and having to re-write it from scratch. This alone should be strong motivation not to plagiarize.

3. *You might be placed on academic probation*—Some colleges and universities automatically place students on academic probation if they are caught being academically dishonest. This could be for as little as one term, or it could last until you complete your degree or leave the institution.

4. *The plagiarism violation might be a permanent part of your academic record*—Colleges and universities can make your dishonesty a permanent part of your scholastic file. This could potentially impact future employment if an organization wants to scrutinize your background. This might never matter . . . but it might also prevent you from getting a job offer.

5. *You might get expelled from the school*—Some colleges and universities have a zero tolerance policy for plagiarism, and this could result in you not being allowed to come back to finish your degree. You might choose to leave a college or university during your academic career, but you do not want to get kicked out.

When can you use this guide?

This book is a must-have anytime you write a paper for college . . . and the type of paper does not matter. Research, essays, reviews, and dissertations all need to be original thinking, unless the sources utilized are properly cited. This guide will help make certain that you do not use others' thoughts and ideas without giving proper credit to the deserving authors.

This guide is divided into six sections as follows:

1. *Plagiarism in General*—Discusses the importance of plagiarism and reasons professors ignore it.

2. *Plagiarism Types*—Names and defines different types of plagiarism.

3. *Plagiarism Examples*—Gives real world examples of each plagiarism type.

4. *Plagiarism Summary*—Summarizes key points of plagiarism.

5. *Plagiarism Review*—Assesses understanding of plagiarism concepts.

6. *Proper Reference Page Citation*—Provides proper APA and MLA citation of books and journals.

Plagiarism in General

Why is plagiarism so important?

Original work needs to be protected for:

Financial reasons—Some people profit monetarily from the work they produce. Plagiarizing their work could affect them and their families monetarily.

Ethical reasons—It is simply not right to take credit for something someone else created. You likely would not want someone using your thoughts or ideas without acknowledgement.

Legal reasons—Copyright laws protect people from plagiarizing others' work. You potentially could end up in the courtroom over academically dishonest actions.

Academic standing reasons—College professors' careers are often based on the original work they produce. *Publish or perish* is alive and well in academia.

Why do some professors ignore plagiarism?

Professors sometime choose to overlook plagiarism because:

It requires more work—Submitting papers to a plagiarism database requires time, and time is often limited, especially if the course is condensed or it is the end of the term when every assignment needs to be graded.

It creates a "teacher vs. learner" mentality—Professors might feel that they are working against students to find cheating, rather than with them to enhance learning. This type of environment can be stressful and difficult because teachers become "offensive" when grading, and students become "defensive" when writing.

The focus shifts from content to originality—Students who put too much emphasis on avoiding plagiarism can lose sight of the importance of content. Some professors might believe that learning is better achieved by *what is said* rather than *how it is said*.

They do not want bad reviews—Students who fail courses typically are not happy, and they might express their discontent through poor instructor evaluations. Bad reviews do not look good for instructors . . . especially when they cannot challenge their rating.

Plagiarism Types

What are the types of plagiarism?

Plagiarism has some very "gray" areas. In other words, it is not always crystal clear what designates plagiarism and what designates legitimate research.

We have classified plagiarism by type so you can get a better understanding of what it entails. These types include *Verbatim Major, Verbatim Minor, Verbatim Plus, Disguise Major, Disguise Minor, Inaccurate, Redundant Major,* and *Redundant Minor.*

Definitions and descriptions of these types are as follows:

Verbatim Major—Copying word for word without source citation.

Example

Original Source

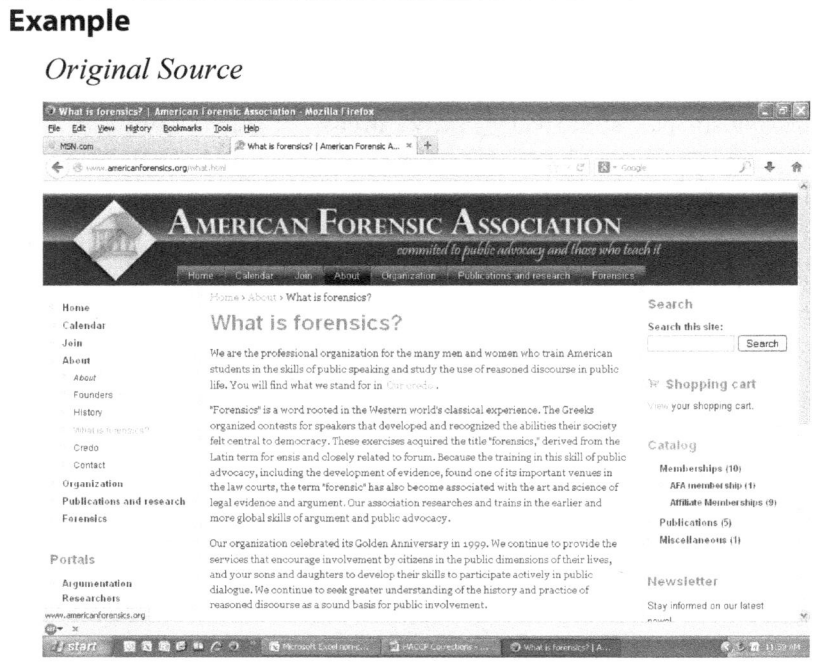

Verbatim Major Plagiarism

"Forensics" is a word rooted in the Western world's classical experience. The Greeks organized contests for speakers that developed and recognized the abilities their society felt central to democracy. These exercises acquired the title "forensics," derived from the Latin term for ensis and closely related to forum. Because the training in this skill of public advocacy, including the development of evidence, found one of its important venues in the law courts, the term "forensic" has also become associated with the art and science of legal evidence and argument.

Explanatory Notes: There is no credit given to the original source (American Forensic Association, 2014) in any form. This is an issue because the student's work appears to be original thinking, when in fact it is not.

Verbatim Minor—Copying word for word with source citation but not designating as a direct quotation.

Example

Original Source

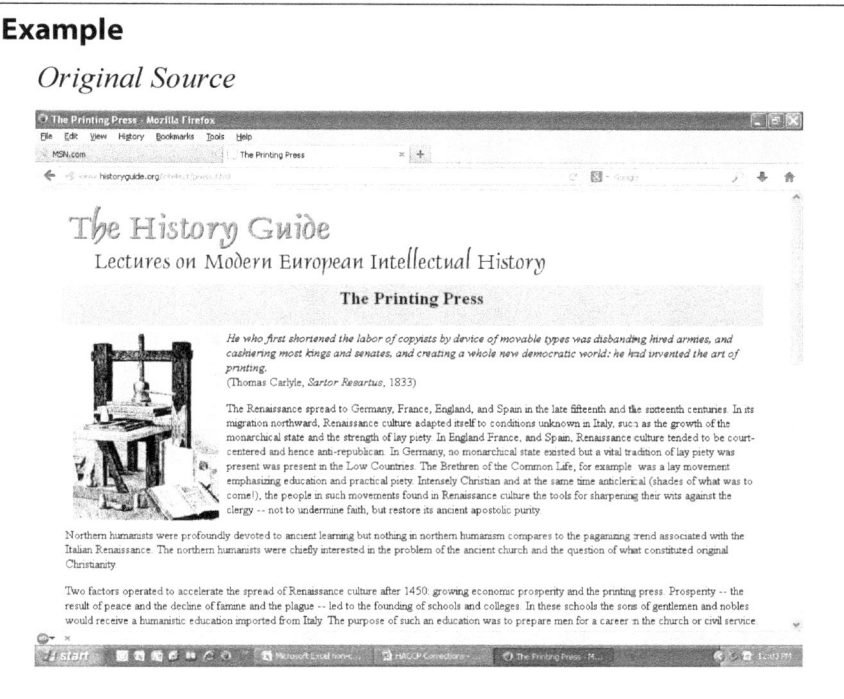

Verbatim Minor Plagiarism

The Renaissance spread to Germany, France, England, and Spain in the late fifteenth and the sixteenth centuries. In its migration northward, Renaissance culture adapted itself to conditions unknown in Italy, such as the growth of the monarchical state and the strength of lay piety. In England France, and Spain, Renaissance culture tended to be court-centered and hence anti-republican. In Germany, no monarchical state existed but a vital tradition of lay piety was present was present in the Low Countries. The Brethren of the Common Life, for example, was a lay movement emphasizing education and practical piety. Intensely Christian and at the same time anticlerical (shades of what was to come!), the people in such movements found in Renaissance culture the tools for sharpening their wits against the clergy—not to undermine faith, but restore its ancient apostolic purity (History Guide, 2014)

Explanatory Notes: Credit is given to the original source, but no credit given as a direct quotation. This is an issue because the student's work appears to be paraphrased, when in fact it is not. APA and MLA guidelines require quotation marks or indentation for direct quotations.

Verbatim Plus—Copying certain portions word for word and inserting some original words with source citation but not designating as a direct quotation.

Example

Original Source

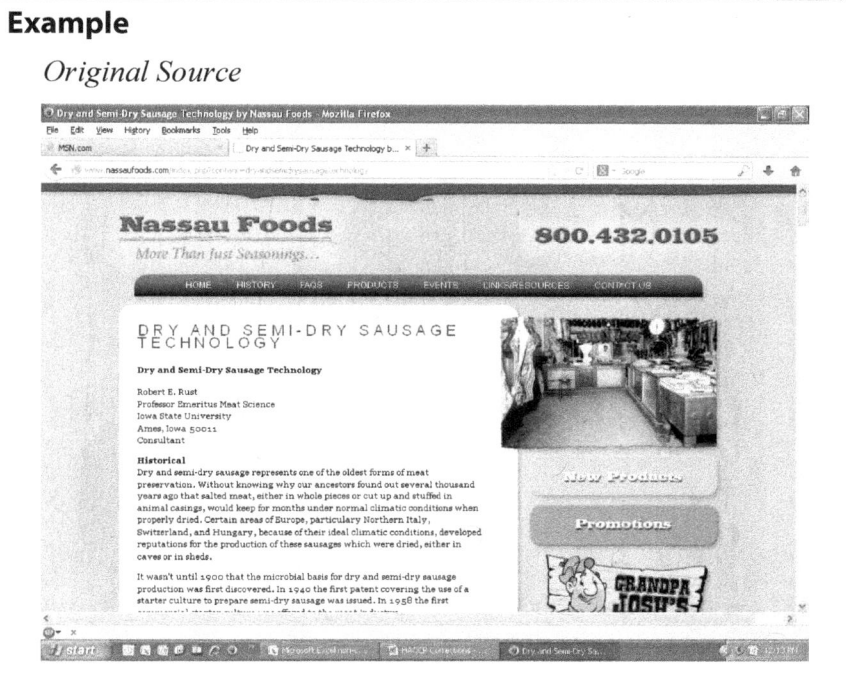

Verbatim Plus

Dry and semi-dry sausage <u>symbolizes</u> one of the oldest forms of <u>preserving meat</u>. Without knowing why our ancestors <u>discovered</u> several thousand years ago that salted meat, either in whole pieces or cut up and stuffed in animal casings, would keep for a <u>long time under</u> normal <u>weather</u> when properly dried (Nassau Foods, 2014).

Explanatory Notes: The underlined words were changed from the original document, but the information is still a direct quotation. Credit is given to the original source, but no credit given as a direct quotation. This is an issue because the student's work appears to be paraphrased, when in fact it is not (except for a few words). APA and MLA guidelines require quotation marks or indentation for direct quotations.

Disguise Major—Changing wording, but keeping the basic content the same without source citation.

Example

Original Source

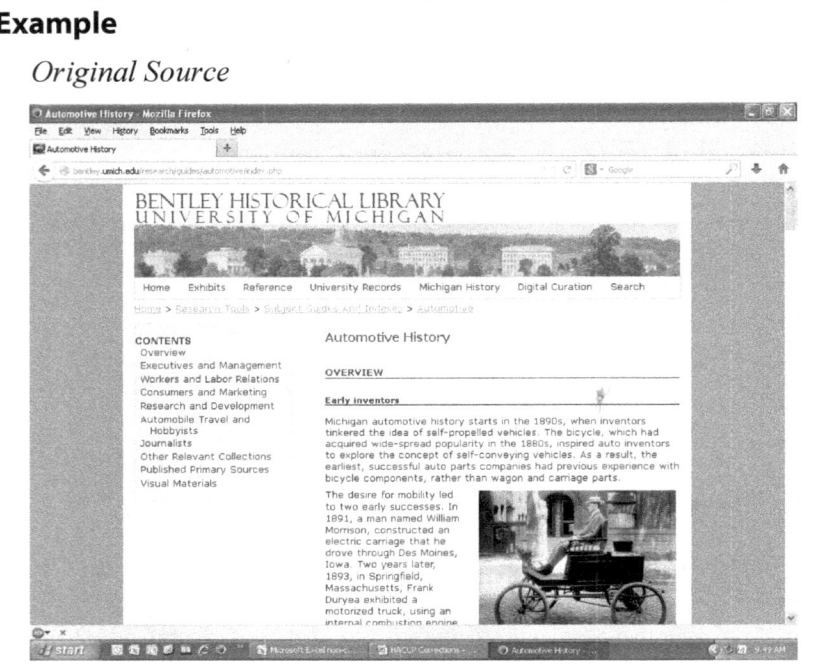

Disguise Major

Michigan automotive history started when inventors began developing motor powered vehicles in the 1890's. These men were inspired by the bicycle, which was now very popular, to explore the idea of self-conveying vehicles. This resulted in the first successful auto parts companies understanding components of bicycles more that those of wagons and carriages.

Explanatory Notes: The wording is not copied; but it is paraphrased, and no credit is given to the original source. This is an issue because the student's work appears to be original thinking, when in fact it is not.

Disguise Minor—Changing wording, but not citing every source.

Example

Original Source #1

Original Source #2

Disguise Minor

After World War I, Adolf Hitler increased Germany's military strength and aligned his country with Japan and Italy in a quest to rule the world. These three nations formed the Axis powers that fought the Allies, consisting of Great Britain, France, and the United States, in World War II (History.com).

Explanatory Notes: The wording is paraphrased, but credit is only given to one source when two sources should be credited. This is an issue because all of the student's work appears to be taken from *History.com*, when in fact some of it is from *Britannica.com*.

Inaccurate—Citing non-existent or inaccurate sources.

Example

Original Source

None.

Inaccurate

Students would rather major in English than Math (Jones, 2013).

Explanatory Notes: Credit is given to an author who does not exist or did not make the statement. While the statement might be true, it needs to be supported with an actual a source that is not made up, taken out of context, or incorrectly referenced.

Redundant Major—Citing sources accurately with original work, but the document was previously submitted for another course.

> **Example**
>
> *Original Source*
>
> A student's paper on organizational communication submitted to BUS 101.
>
> *Redundant Major*
>
> The same paper on organizational communication submitted by the same student to COM 112.
>
> *Explanatory Notes:* Students are expected to create original work for every class they take, unless their college or university designates otherwise. This student submitted the same paper for two different courses, so the second submission falls under academic dishonesty.

Redundant Minor—Citing sources accurately, but there is little or no original work. This is not necessarily plagiarism, but it is a form of academic dishonesty because the student did not add value to what has already been researched or written.

> **Example**
>
> *Original Source*
>
> A student's 12-page paper consisted of 95% direct quotations. All direct quotations are properly cited.
>
> *Redundant Minor*
>
> While the citations are correct, there is very little original work. The 12-page document amounts to less than one page of original thinking by the student.
>
> *Explanatory Notes:* Colleges and universities expect students to submit original work for courses. A 12-page paper consisting of over 11 pages of direct quotations indicates academic dishonesty on the part of the student because the vast majority of the work is not original.

Plagiarism Examples

What are some real examples of plagiarism in the classroom?

The following are true examples of academic dishonesty (names and courses have been changed).

1. Verbatim Major

James was enrolled in a graduate program at the same college where he received his bachelor's degree. He submitted a research paper for an assignment that was found by a plagiarism database to contain over 70% text copied word for word from the Internet. James rarely gave credit to the deserving authors, and he never gave them credit as a direct quotation.

As should be expected, James' instructor failed him for plagiarism. James was irate when he received the failing grade. He sent his instructor a threatening email using a variety of derogatory terms and threatening innuendos. His instructor felt intimidated and forwarded the email to the graduate school dean, who contacted James.

The dean tried to explain the seriousness of plagiarism and to comprehend James' understanding of academic dishonesty. James, however, refused to listen. Instead, he voiced his displeasure with the college and the dean for receiving a failing grade, again using personal insults and verbally aggressive language.

The dean did not change James' grade. James not only failed the course for plagiarism, he was also expelled from the graduate school due to the threatening nature of his email to his instructor and his conversation with the dean.

Unfortunately, James never believed he was guilty of plagiarism. He spent a lot of time on his paper and believed that his effort should have been rewarded. He would not acknowledge the fact that he was academically dishonest, and only focused on the amount of effort he put forth to complete the assignment.

Lesson learned: Plagiarism inflicts damage upon people and institutions. The student, teacher, dean, and school were ultimately affected in a negative way. The student was kicked out of a university, the teacher and dean were intimidated due to personal insults and threats, and the school lost a paying customer.

2. Verbatim Minor

Jennifer was less than 10 credits short of finishing her undergraduate degree, and she took a class that required writing a paper on organizational communication. Her instructor submitted the paper to a plagiarism database which found that 69% of the paper was copied material. In every instance, the copied text gave credit to the deserving authors, but never in the form of a direct quotation. Credit was always issued in the form of paraphrasing.

Jennifer's instructor failed her based on the plagiarism detection website findings. Jennifer could not understand why she failed because she always gave credit to the sources she used. She did not think it mattered that the credit she gave was in the form of paraphrasing rather than as a direct quotation. After all, the deserving authors were receiving credit for their work; so why is this simple deviation from writing style guidelines a plagiarism issue?

The reason Jennifer failed is because it looked like she paraphrased someone else's work, when in fact she copied and pasted it. It takes much more time and effort to rewrite someone else's work than it does to copy and paste it; and that is why writing style manuals, such as APA and MLA, have specific guidelines in place for direct quotations.

Jennifer went to the administration at her university and appealed the grade. The administration backed the instructor's action and said the only way she could pass the course is if the instructor were to voluntarily change the grade. The instructor refused to change the grade in order to be fair to those students who submit original work with proper citation and to uphold the integrity of the university.

Lesson learned: Copying and pasting direct quotations without proper citation violates academic honesty. Plagiarism in this case was real . . . and so were the academic consequences.

3. Verbatim Plus

Noelle was working on an associate degree and took a course on medical technology. She chose to write her final paper on brain stents and found all the information she needed on various medical websites. She copied information from these websites but made sure she changed some words to avoid copying and pasting all of the information. She then gave credit to the deserving authors in the form of paraphrasing.

After receiving Noelle's paper, her instructor submitted it to a plagiarism database. That site found over 80% of the document was copied from websites. Within every copied paragraph, there were three or four original words, but the rest of the text was copied. Some sentences contained no original wording.

Noelle gave credit to the authors of the original words in the form of paraphrasing, but her instructor still gave her a failing grade. He did this because she gave the false appearance that she paraphrased her work, when in fact the majority of it was copied and pasted from the Internet.

Noelle was obviously unhappy about her failing grade, but she accepted it after her instructor explained his reasoning. She lost credit for the course and had to take another class in place of it in order to receive her associate degree.

Lesson learned: Inserting a few original words in a copied document does not warrant a paraphrasing citation because the majority of the information is still a direct quotation. If the majority of the work being cited is a direct quotation, then cite it as such to prevent being accused of taking credit for rewording someone else's work when it was actually copied.

4. Disguise Major

Tammy was a student in a geology course at a community college. One of her assignments involved writing a paper on volcanic eruptions. She needed to research the reasons why they occur and whether they can be prevented.

Tammy found the information she needed online and also in her textbook and subsequently completed the assignment. Her instructor submitted her paper to a plagiarism database which detected less than 4% was copied material.

The lack of plagiarism evidence looked good for Tammy. However, the instructor noticed that there were only two sources cited as references in the document. This seemed very peculiar for a 12-page document, so he decided to investigate further.

Upon closer examination, the instructor noticed that much of the information appeared to be very similar to designated reading assignments in the course textbook. The information was re-worded, but credit was not given to any authors' in the vast majority of instances. This made it appear as if the work was Tammy's original thinking, when it actually stemmed from other author's thoughts and ideas. The plagiarism database did not detect copied material because the course textbook was a print version only, and it had never been entered into the database.

Tammy's instructor gave her an F for the course. She was upset and appealed the grade to the dean of her college, but lost her case due to academic dishonesty. She did not receive credit for the course and ultimately had to repeat it the next semester.

Lesson learned: Rewording someone else's work without giving them credit is a form of plagiarism. If you change wording, but keep the same basic content, then you must cite the source in the form of paraphrasing.

5. Disguise Minor

Max enrolled in an English course that was required for completion of his undergraduate degree. For one of his assignments, he wrote a paper on high school spelling issues and submitted it to his instructor.

The instructor submitted Max's paper to a plagiarism database which detected there was 41% copied material. The copied material was found throughout the document, but it was typically only a few words at a time. This indicated the information utilized in Max's paper was paraphrased, not copied as a direct quotation.

The paraphrased information was referenced in every paragraph, so this looked good for Max. However, the plagiarism database indicated that often times there were three sources utilized; but only one of them was cited. Max heavily paraphrased two authors in his paper that were never given credit for their work. Instead, a third author was cited as being the only source.

Based on the instructor's finding, Max failed the course. He was upset about the situation, but decided not to appeal his final grade and risk further academic punishment if he lost.

Ultimately, Max had to repeat the course in order to graduate. This meant that he had to pay twice for the same three credits. At $430 per credit hour, it ended up costing him an additional $1,290.

Lesson learned: Issuing credit to one author for another author's work is a form of plagiarism that can have severe consequences. All sources used in a paper need to be cited.

6. Inaccurate

Raymond was enrolled in a sociology course and wrote a paper on rural poverty. His instructor submitted it to a plagiarism database, and it found less than 5% was copied material. This looked good to the instructor, but she recognized very few of the authors cited in the document. This seemed a bit odd since the instructor had taught college sociology courses and conducted related research for over 20 years, so she decided to investigate.

Her investigation found that seven of the nine references cited in Raymond's paper were fictitious. All of the books and journals were legitimate, but the authors and articles were fabricated so they could be used as support for Raymond's arguments. He probably could have found research that backed his thinking, but he chose to take the easy way out by making up his references.

Raymond's instructor failed him for academic dishonesty. He was fully aware that he gave credit to fictitious authors and accepted her F grade without challenge. He also had to repeat the course because it was required for him to graduate. This meant that he had to pay for the same course twice.

Lesson learned: Never support your arguments or thinking with sources that do not exist. This form of academic dishonesty might not be caught be plagiarism databases, but it can be noticed by experienced teachers. The use of fictitious sources can cost you grades, time, and money.

7. Redundant Major

In the summer between his junior and senior years, Mike took a business management course. He had to write a paper on leadership, and he chose business ethics as his topic. After he turned in the paper, his instructor submitted it to a plagiarism database which found less than 2% was copied information. The paper was original, well written, and adhered to required APA guidelines. Mike received an A grade for his work.

The following fall Mike enrolled in a business ethics course. This course required students to write a paper on leadership ethics. Mike decided to use the same paper he had written for the summer management course for this assignment. When his instructor submitted the paper to a plagiarism database, it found that 100% of the paper was copied.

Mike's instructor failed him based on plagiarism. She referred him to the academic honesty section of her syllabus that stated students could not submit a paper to her class that they had already submitted for another course.

Mike was very upset after receiving an F for the course. How could she fail him for plagiarism? It was his work, and everything was properly referenced. He did not copy anything from anyone other than himself, and why should he be punished for that?

He decided to appeal the grade to his college. He submitted all the information he had available and thought he had the necessary support to get his grade changed. He argued that he did not plagiarize because it was his original work.

The college did not support Mike. He lost his appeal because the instructor had "no submissions from other courses" written in the syllabus, and he was forced to repeat the course the following term.

Lesson learned: Submitting the same paper for two different courses is a form of plagiarism if the instructor does not allow it. Many colleges and universities expect students to create new work for every course, so check with your teacher or school for rules regarding same paper submission.

8. Redundant Minor

Stephanie took an anthropology course and needed to write a paper on Asian customs. She went to the Internet and found a wealth of information on this topic. She used many direct quotations from her web sources and was diligent about making sure they were properly cited.

Stephanie submitted her paper to her instructor, and he uploaded it to a plagiarism database. That website determined that over 95% of the 12-page document was copied from the Internet. The instructor reviewed her paper in more detail and found that the copied information was all direct quotations. However, these direct quotations were not plagiarized because they were cited properly.

The instructor failed Stephanie for excessive use of direct quotations. The quotations were properly cited, so nothing was plagiarized; but there was very little original work. Lack of original work is sometimes considered to be academically dishonest because students are expected to add value to their writing by injecting their own thoughts and ideas.

Stephanie accepted her final grade and did not challenge her instructor via the college's administration. Had she done so, it is difficult to determine what their ruling would have been because she did not plagiarize . . . but she also did very little original work. However, if the instructor had a direct quotation limit in his syllabus (20% for example), then she likely would have lost the appeal.

Lesson learned: Submitting a paper that consists of mostly direct quotations is considered academically dishonest by some professors, colleges, and universities. Don't take the risk . . . think and write originally to avoid jeopardizing your grade. Also, be sure to review your instructor's syllabus to see if limits have been imposed on direct quotations. It's better to be safe than sorry.

9. Unique

This story is the most interesting because the author did not plagiarize.

Yvonne needed only two more classes to complete her MBA. Her GPA was above a 3.5, and she was thought of by her teachers and the school as an excellent student. She also worked full time as a trainer in the human resources department of a Fortune 500 company. Part of her job involved lecturing on workplace diversity.

A course she was enrolled in required her to write a paper on diversity. This appeared to be a topic she understood well, so it came as no surprise that her finished paper was detailed, informative, and well-written. However, a plagiarism detection website found that her paper was 68% copied from another student's work at a different institution.

Yvonne's instructor failed her for plagiarism. She emailed the instructor and told him she could not understand how this work was plagiarized because it was her original thoughts and ideas. She explained that the information in her paper was written by her and used in her diversity lectures at work.

The instructor believed Yvonne might be telling the truth, but her work was found to be copied; so he told her she needed to contact the graduate school in order to get the grade changed.

Yvonne met with the dean of the graduate school and pleaded her case. She brought proof of her lectures and had her employer write a letter of support.

The dean also believed Yvonne was being honest, so she decided to conduct an investigation. She obtained the name of the student who supposedly wrote the original work, and then things started to make sense.

The student was actually in the audience during one of Yvonne's lectures. He copied one of her handouts and turned it into a paper, which he submitted for an assignment he had at Palomino State College. His instructor turned the paper into the plagiarism database, which found it all to be original.

In reality, the student's work was not original, but it had never been submitted to a plagiarism database. When Yvonne's work was submitted to the plagiarism database, it was found to be 68% copied because the student from Palomino State College submitted the work first.

Yvonne's grade was reversed from an F to an A. She did not need to repeat the course and graduated on schedule.

This situation is very interesting. It appeared to be a sure case of plagiarism, but Yvonne's work was original. Someone copied her lecture and got away with submitting it for original work because it was not in the plagiarism database.

Lesson learned: Be careful during lectures, presentations, and training because there might be some unethical people in the audience who want to take credit for your original work. Let them know that the material is expressly yours, and they cannot use it without your written permission. You might even consider copyrighting your work if you believe it could be plagiarized by others.

Plagiarism in Summary

When can you plagiarize and not be held accountable?

The simple answer is NEVER. You can't copy "just a little" information and assume it is alright. Authors of original work need to be credited for their efforts, and you need to provide that credit when you write.

There is, however, an exception to this rule. Common knowledge and facts are not considered plagiarized and do not have to be cited. Common knowledge and facts are information that is known to anyone who reads, watches TV, listens to the radio, or holds conversations with other human beings. Examples include:

- *Barack Obama was elected president of the United States of America.*

  However, if you state that Barack Obama was elected president in 2008 because his staff understood the needs of the American public based on research they did using statistical data from The Democratic National Committee, then you should cite a source.

- *Barry Sanders played football for the Detroit Lions.*

  However, if you state that Barry Sanders retired from the Detroit Lions with 15,269 rushing yards and 109 touchdowns, then you should cite a source.

Deciding whether or not something is common knowledge or a fact can be difficult. If you are concerned that you might be plagiarizing, then cite the source. Be concerned so you don't get burned!

The acronym *DODGE* can be used for avoiding academically dishonest writing:

D—Don't copy and paste information from websites without citation as a direct quotation.

O—Open your mind to potential sources of plagiarism. Tables, pictures, and graphs that are copied need to give credit to the deserving author(s).

D—Don't assume you are not plagiarizing someone else's work. When in doubt, point it out!

G—Get help if you need it. Ask your college or university because some institutions issue specific rules and guidelines for plagiarism.

E—Establish lifelong habits for avoiding plagiarism. Rules for plagiarizing extend beyond the walls of academia. Your work career could also be adversely affected by dishonest writing.

Dodge the plagiarism bullet and avoid jeopardizing your grade and good academic standing.

What is the future of plagiarism?

It will likely become more important than it is today. As the Internet becomes an ever increasingly popular choice for finding sources, the consequences for academic dishonesty will likely be more severe. Almost anyone can copy and paste other people's work from a website, but it takes much more effort to incorporate that work into a composition that uses it as support while bestowing proper credit to the deserving authors.

Plagiarism summary—dos and don'ts

Do

- Cite all deserving authors for their work
- Cite direct quotations as direct quotations
- Cite summaries as paraphrasing
- Check with your school for specific rules regarding academic dishonesty

Don't

- Submit the same paper for different classes (unless approved by the instructor or school)
- Assume you only copied a little bit so it does not have to be properly cited
- Use sources that do not exist or are improperly referenced
- Use a high percentage of direct quotations

Plagiarism Review

1. True or False

   a. Plagiarism should be avoided in academia and your work career after graduation.

   b. Making up sources is a form of academic dishonesty.

   c. Direct quotations do not need to be cited as such if they are less than 100 words.

   d. Submitting the same paper for two different courses is acceptable if the courses are in different departments.

   e. Legal concerns are one reason that original work needs to be protected.

   f. Rules for academic honesty are the same at every college and university.

   g. Copying and pasting information from a website without proper citation is only considered plagiarism if that information is from a scholarly book or educational journal.

   h. Using information from a source without citation is acceptable if you change a few words.

2. Choose the Correct Answer

   a. Copying word for word should be cited as *paraphrasing/a direct quotation.*

   b. Plagiarism is a form of *academic dishonesty/reference citation.*

   c. *Inaccurate/Verbatim Minor* plagiarism entails citing non-existent or inaccurate sources.

   d. *Statistics/common knowledge and facts* are exceptions to academic dishonesty and can be listed without a source.

   e. *Plagiarism databases/government websites* detect academic dishonesty in student papers.

   f. Always review your instructor's syllabus to see if limits have been imposed on *direct quotations/paraphrasing.*

g. Original work needs to be protected for *cultural/ethical* reasons.

h. Some professors overlook plagiarism because *it creates extra work/they approve of it.*

Examples: Proper Reference Page Citations

In this section, basic examples are provided for proper citation of books and journals on the reference page of a paper using APA (6th edition) and MLA (7th edition) writing styles. Please note that references for both writing styles should be double spaced, but they are single spaced in this book to save space.

APA (6th edition)

Reprinted From *APA: The Easy Way!* with permission from the authors.

Books (no author and no editor)

Communication in the workplace. (2014). Cambridge, NJ: Boston Books.

Books (no author and one editor)

Dewa, P. (Ed.). (2013). *Chess strategies made simple.* New York, NY: Davidson Books.

Books (one author)

Schreck, E. P. (2012). *Mistakes of supervising a culturally diverse workforce in the USDA.* Boston, MA: Corrigan Books.

Books (two authors)

Jones, T., Timocco, M., & Smith, R. L. (2013). *Fire prevention at home.* Philadelphia, PA: Johannesburg Books.

Books (three to seven authors)

Sienkiewicz, J. H., Scarcelli, T. A., & Alexandrowicz, M. P. (2014). *Great high school athletes transition into coaching roles.* Clawson, MI: Roddy Press.

Books (eight or more authors)

Partz, M., Mentro, J. P., Harcelli, T., Banshi, P. P., Cretzell, G., Smith, C. E., . . . Sauls, C. E. (2013). A qualitative study of modern Native American dance. *Journal of Dance Methodology, 12*(3), 12–21.

Online or Electronic Books (DOI, eReader, or Internet)

Andrantis, J. (2013). *Teaching issues in middle schools* [Adobe Digital Editions version]. doi:10.1067/006967332A

DeGeller, M. J. (2014). *Bond investing: Modern strategies* [Kindle DX version]. Retrieved from http://www.amazon.com/bond- inv/ dp/16535roge=ebook.us

Rusholt, J. P. (2014). *Health insurance for teacher unions: Reaching a compromise.* Retrieved from http://www.onlineinsurancebooks. net/schools.asp?itemLP=14

Journals (one author)

Harcourt, J. (2008). The influence of peer pressure on dating within the same group of friends. *Journal of Social Interaction, 55,* 312–319.

Journals (multiple authors)

Partz, M., Mentro, J. P., Harcelli, T., Banshi, P. P., Cretzell, G., Smith, C. E., . . . Sauls, C. E. (2008). A qualitative study of modern Native American dance. *Journal of Dance Methodology, 12*(3), 12–21.

Online or Electronic Journals (DOI, eReader, or Internet)

Ostroff, C. (2002). The relationship between satisfaction, attitudes, and performance: An organizational level analysis. *Journal of Applied Psychology, 12*(2), 963–974. doi:10:2114-445.57.291

DeGeller, M. J. (2010). *Bond investing: Modern strategies* [Kindle DX version]. Retrieved from http://www.amazon.com/bond-inv/dp/16535roge=ebook.us

Griffeth, R. W., Hom, P. W., & Gaertner, S. (2004). A meta-analysis of antecedents and correlates of employee turnover. Update, moderator tests, and research implications for the next millennium. *Journal of Management, 26*(3), 463–476. Retrieved from http://www.nwlink.com/~donplark/ leader/learnor2.html

MLA (8th edition)

Reprinted from *MLA: The Easy Way!* with permission from the authors.

Books (no author and one editor)

Frank, Donald, ed. *From Past to Present: Forty Years of Sound Distribution Advice.* Chicago: Random, 2015.

Books (one author)

Hoban, Donna M. *Medical Methodology for Combating Migraine Headaches.* Houghton Books, 2015.

Books (multiple authors use et al.)

Sienkiewicz, John Henry, et al. *Great High School Athletes Transition into Coaching Roles.* Harper, 2015.

Online Books

Diegel, Karen, and Lisa Shankie. *Socialist Perspectives on War*, 2014. *United Women for Justice*. Edited by Janet LaLonde, 2014. U. of Oregon, www.uo.edu/forc/ddt/9980/td.

Journals (one author)

Mickelberry, Claude Charles. "A Comparative Analysis of Leadership Styles." *Leadership Quarterly*, vol. 13, no. 2, June 2013, pp. 12+.

Journals (multiple authors)

LeFrank, Kathleen L., et al. "The Influence of High School Relationships on Adulthood Friendships." *Journal of Social Commentary*, vol. 21, 2013, pp. 119–32.

CD (Periodically Published Database)

Hennessy, John Thomas. "Native Americans and Teams: Qualitative Research in a Northern Michigan Casino." *Journal of Social Norms*, vol. 21, 2014, pp. 125–29. *Periodical Abstracts* Ondisc. UMI-Proquest. Apr. 2014.

Sound Recordings

Ellington, Duke, conductor. *Concert For the Philippines*. Duke Ellington Orchestra. Recorded 13 Feb. 1945. Columbia, 1979.

Seger, Bob. *Bob Seger's Greatest Rock Ballads*. Capitol, 2014.

Wilkerson, Lynn. *The Evolution of Music*. Performed by Andrew Folin and Kyle Clemmons. EMI, 1978.

King, B. B. "Rollin' Stones." Recorded 12 May 1956. *King of Blues*. Chess, 2015.

Film or Videos

Living For Tomorrow. Directed by Mitchell Shockey. Performed by David Reed, Christopher Cadjun, Tia Presnal, and Paul Gellstone. Miramax, 2013.

Performance (concert, opera, ballet, or play)

Hamlet. By William Shakespeare. Directed by Dennis Hartsig. Performed by Michael Donnell and Angela Wilmer. Magic Bag Theater, 5 Apr. 2014.

Answer Key

True or False

a. True—plagiarism can be detrimental to you as a student and as an employee.

b. True—you are falsely establishing support by using a resource that does not exist.

c. False—all direct quotations need to be cited, regardless of length.

d. False—submitting papers for two different courses is only acceptable if the professor, college, or university says it is acceptable.

e. True—legality is important in academia and the real world.

f. False—academic honesty rules may differ between schools.

g. False—information copied and pasted from any website must be properly cited.

h. False—all information used needs to be cited if you are citing someone else's thoughts or ideas.

Choose the Correct Answer

a. a direct quotation—paraphrasing involves summarizing

b. academic dishonesty—reference citation involves citing sources in text and in the reference section

c. inaccurate—Verbatim Minor plagiarism involves copying word with source citation but not designating as a direct quotation.

d. common knowledge and facts—statistics need the source cited

e. Plagiarism databases—the government does not supply websites for this purpose

f. direct quotations—instructor typically do not put limitations on paraphrasing

g. ethical—culture is not a major concern for protecting original work

h. it creates extra work—professors never approve of students plagiarizing other's work.